HISTORIES OF DESIRE

Work by Ron Butlin

POETRY

Stretto (Outline Arts, 1976)
Creatures Tamed by Cruelty (Edinburgh University SPB, 1979)
The Exquisite Instrument (Salamander Press, 1982)
Ragtime in Unfamiliar Bars (Secker & Warburg, 1985)
Histories of Desire (Bloodaxe Books, 1995)

FICTION

The Tilting Room (Canongate, 1983)
The Sound of My Voice (Canongate and Paladin, 1987; revised edition Black Ace Books, 1994)

PLAYS

The Music Box (performed at Aberlour, 1985)
We've Been Had (Faceback Theatre Company, 1986)
Blending In, after Michel Vinaver (Traverse Theatre for Edinburgh Fringe, 1989; adapted for Radio 3, 1990)

OPERA LIBRETTI

Markheim (Occasional Opera Company, 1990)
Dark Kingdom (Paragon Opera Project, 1992)

RON BUTLIN

Histories of Desire

BLOODAXE BOOKS

Copyright © Ron Butlin 1995

ISBN: 1 85224 339 2

First published 1995 by
Bloodaxe Books Ltd,
P.O. Box 1SN,
Newcastle upon Tyne NE99 1SN.

Bloodaxe Books Ltd acknowledges
the financial assistance of Northern Arts.

LEGAL NOTICE
All rights reserved. No part of this book may be
reproduced, stored in a retrieval system, or
transmitted in any form, or by any means, electronic,
mechanical, photocopying, recording or otherwise,
without prior written permission from Bloodaxe Books Ltd.

Requests to publish work from this book
must be sent to Bloodaxe Books Ltd.

Ron Butlin has asserted his right under
Section 77 of the Copyright, Designs and Patents Act 1988
to be identified as the author of this work.

Cover printing by J. Thomson Colour Printers Ltd, Glasgow.

Printed in Great Britain by
Cromwell Press Ltd, Broughton Gifford, Melksham, Wiltshire.

for Regi

Acknowledgements

Acknowledgements are due to the editors of the following publications in which some of these poems first appeared: *The Best of Scottish Poetry* (Chambers, 1989), *The Big Issue in Scotland*, *Carapace* (South Africa), *Cencrastus*, *Chapman*, *Cinq-plus Dimanche* (Mauritius), *The Dark Horse*, *Dienovidzio* (Lithuania), *Edinburgh Review*, *Encounter*, *Familia* (Romania), *Fox*, *Literatura Ukrania* (Ukraine), *New Edinburgh Review*, *New Writing Scotland*, *orte* (Switzerland), *Poetry Book Society Christmas Supplement* (PBS/Hutchinson, 1986), *Poetry Review*, *The Scotsman*, *Six Poètes Écossais* (Telo Martius, 1992), *Under Cover* (Mainstream Publishing, 1993), *Verse* and *With Both Feet off the Ground* (Dumfries and Galloway Libraries, 1993). Several poems were broadcast by BBC Radio 3, Mauritius Broadcasting Corporation, Radio Clyde, and Radio Scotland.

I would like to thank the Scottish Arts Council for a Writer's Bursary; also Midlothian District Council Libraries Department, and the University of Stirling who have allowed me time to complete this book.

Contents

11	Coming of Age
12	Near Linton Burnfoot
13	At Linton Kirk
14	Beginnings of the Ice Age
15	Histories of Desire
16	The Painting Lesson
17	The Start of the Affair
18	Don Juan at Forty
20	Our Last Night in Africa
22	Flic-en-Flac
23	African Sunlight
24	Budapest: All Wars Are Civil Wars
25	An Incident in Paris
26	The Lake at Preda
27	Barcelona: August Tenth
28	What I Remember Most
30	Advertisement for a Scottish Servant
31	One Life
32	Today
33	A Final Word on the Dream-house
34	The Shadow-sailor
35	The Landscape We Live In
36	Lifeline
37	A Ballad: In My House
38	Edinburgh: A Place of My Own
40	Prayer
41	Day and Night
42	The Present King of France
46	Three Biographies
48	Letting the Demons Speak
54	Ryecroft

Coming of Age

You're waiting for a train that isn't late,
or glancing out the window at the street
before the curtain's pulled.

Some broken glass, a child's ball bouncing
down a flight of steps, the threat of
rain, a ploughed field,
the colour of a passing car –
each in turn betrays the man you are.

Take care, your heartbeat's stilled
and still you do not die. No delegate
can take your place or answer to your name:
when the curtain's closed the world's shut out.
Your train arrives on time.

Near Linton Burnfoot

Tarred roads, metal cattle-grids and wheeltracks mesh
so tightly no land can escape; tractor ruts
cut deep into the grass to cross and double-stitch
the fields together; where the high ground pushes upwards,
pylons rigid with electricity stand guard
upon the hills. Bridges staple running water,
lines of fence-posts nail the valley sides in place.

Rain and ploughed mud. Rooks' cries claw the air;
a banshee trapped in corrugated iron shrieks
to be released. Trees grasp at nothing and let go –
a thousand masts rammed deep into one deck, and yet
the countryside remains becalmed. It is a scene
a child has painted splashing colours on sodden paper:
his carelessness might tear a mountainside apart.

Shingle being ground to nothing on the river-bed,
the clouds' silence soaking into the hills –
these are secrets I dare not tell
even to myself. They weight each moment of my life.

At Linton Kirk

Linton Kirk is stone and timber hollowed out of air
where stained glass, darkening to a patch of shadow, traces out
a present tense across the floor.

Our first weekend together: a night without much sleep,
a morning's levitation over hills and cold rain.
The visitors' book lies open. We flip the pages back
to catch sight of a world before we'd met,
then pause uncertain what to write. I glance outside:

an east wind scours the burnt yellow fields to black,
tearing colour from trees; the blunted edge of winter sunlight
hacks at names, dates and words of consolation;
the dead withdraw into the living.

Your scent, the colour of the scarf you wear,
our closeness – these are not memories.
Once we've signed the book and put the date we'll leave
and Linton Kirk stand empty.
How far into the future can I reach to take your hand?

Beginnings of the Ice Age

An ocean hardens into Linton Valley as line
on line the winter geese fly south – tidemarks
on a farther shore.

The ocean's freezing over: wind, scratching its surface
here and there, suggests what might have been.
Someone's voice, another's glance, the taste a woman's skin has
as she wakes – all these remain, and are
the brittleness of shells.

The geese trail silence after them until the shoreline
disappears. This is the ground we stand on –
dark sand and darker water.
A rowan tree takes root beside our house;
a stone bridge hump-backs over Linton burn;
the hill we'd planned to walk across today
is turning green. Creation of the world seems easier
than a change of heart.

Histories of Desire

That was when I threw the stone and then ran after;
splashing into Smallholme burn I made the colours
of a summer's day cascade around me.
That was when the water stilled to rowanberries,
clouds and dark green leaves I could never reach
before. I tried to pick one up –
that was when the earth and sky first slipped
between my fingers.

All histories are histories of desire, they tell me
how my life begins and ends: a stretch of water,
a stone a child sends skimming
to the other side.

The Painting Lesson

Your sticky fingerprints smear the falling rain
then prod a river into place. You smile at me:
'Your turn now.'

Thumbs first, so as not to make a mess
I press a set of ten neat circles endlessly
shut in, across the page.

You shake your head, tilt the paper – and the colours run.
At my fingertips you show me unknown solar systems spinning
into unknown skies, and whirlpools
roaring to the centre of the earth.

The Start of the Affair

Let's tear the moon in half and keep the darker side.
Turn out the light.

(Shadows of a man and woman touch and then let go –
these, the only truths they know,
are trapped between the only words they dare not say.)

Turn out the light but do not turn away,
one fragment of the moon brings night.
Its ragged light is all we have to see by.

Don Juan at Forty

1

There isn't time for every clip-on bow
and straight. You're late. Wait –
and you'll get left behind.
Accelerate –
or die. Now, pick a tie –
but not that cross-check wreck. You blind?
Your new shirt's double-fluted ripples flow
against it; tartan's even worse. You'd like to wear
the birthday-cufflinks, centre-part your hair,
risk the two-tone shoes? OK, then choose. And no
half measures. You've reached your fortieth year –
it's time to put your trousers on and show
the world who's master here.

Another tie? Let's try this Paisley-patterned swirl
of calloused colours, curves and broken nerves –
and knot it tight. Here's the mirror. Right: full-frontal/
profile. *Tighter*. The birthday-boy deserves
the birthday-best. That's *your* reflection pressed against the glass –
press back to steady it. Such moments pass.
Ready? Deep breath, chest out, turn, step *one*
and *two* and *three*. The door. The landing. Stairs.
Breathe deeper. Good, now grip the rail – and *ten* – don't run –
eleven, twelve – let go the rail – and there's
your guests assembled. Smile. It's time to mingle
picking out which women might be single.

Cough for silence. Speech. Your few words say
how deeply moved you are: that done you turn away.
Romantic overtures for two, played by ear,
begin: you know the score by heart and sound sincere
even to yourself. Your grace-notes whisper sweet,
sweet nothings. Only lesser artists need deceive –
what you say becomes at once what you believe.

Look across into the mirror, *there*:
Don Juan at forty, the man with thinning hair,
in syncopation with himself alone,
a virtuoso doomed to solo on
and on towards the loneliest harmonic...
But see he's found a partner, modulated into tonic
doubling on gin to toast their new duet
(set in two-part harmony to let
his smiles and well-timed glances emphasise
the hidden theme). His heartbeat bass-line plays
its two-note phrase *staccato* as he lays
a hand upon her arm. He talks: he tries
'philosophy', then 'feelings'. What's left unsaid
suggests a taxi home, more drinks, then bed...

But here's a husband. Smile. Firm handshake, birthday
greetings tendered and accepted. Once more
the whole world's someone else's wife – her sympathy
and closeness starved by you into desire.
More drinks. Let's offer round the tray of cheese-squares,
dips and olives – the picked-at sticks and stones
are worth a joke about mortality.

2

After midnight and alone. You still have time to part
the curtains, stare into the dark, possess the stars –
their distant chillness cannot touch your heart
for long. So, lock the windows, doors, the bolts and bars,
snib what can be snibbed. If not love,
then some remembrance of who you are endures –
without, each man condemns himself to prove
the dreams he lives by. These dreams are yours:
they dress you, move your right foot forward,
then your left, prompt your every word...

Here is your empty bed.
Switch off the light and do not be afraid.

Our Last Night in Africa
(for Randall)

I bargained for an inch-high king,
his queen, their servants and musicians worked
in bronze. *A good price for you, my friend.*
Special good price.
The souvenir that I'd been looking for.

*

Night curtained off the whole of Africa
with one quick tug.

Insects hissed us back to our hotel.

We washed, ate. An old man shuffled to our table
when the prostitutes gave up.
Onto the heavy linen cloth (the only green
we'd seen for days) he laid a clumsy-looking bangle,
invited us to feel its weight.

See, my gentlemen, please see.
He sat an hour with us and hardly spoke:
There were no words for where his village stood;
None for how the sun became imprisoned in him,
and will not rise.

*

Our fan is broken. I cannot sleep. I've come downstairs:
the fountain's been switched off, the plastic chairs are stacked
in silhouette, the electricity's cut.
Still-life: 'Central Hotel, Kano (only a taxi-ride
from the Sahara)'. The courtyard's breathless heat
and darkness sketched as moonlight
(that same shade of metal-grey the old man placed
before us). This after-tint reveals
its hidden detail:

the line of men, women and children
each one with a bangle hammered
to their wrist. There's no room on the page
to show what happened next.

Our last night in Africa –

Rubbing out the moon I find what's nailed there
in its place.

Flic-en-Flac

A yellow bird pecks at Mauritius island, then flies off.
The concrete paddle-steamer we're staying in has run aground.
The jungle round us has been cleared for re-flotation, litter
and mosquito pools of rain.

Our half-completed steamboat (minus paddle-wheel
and smokestack) sinks up to its windowsills
in sand. A voyage of pure speculation:
land values rising by 50% per annum.

We spend our evenings small-game hunting in our room.
Every morning we re-discover red, gold, green
and silver-striped fish browsing upon the silence
of underwater trees.

Midday: the smallest particle of sun breaks off to settle
once again upon its own shadow. *Peck-peck-
peck:* while twenty yards away the jungle rots, feeds
and grows without harvest, without season.

African Sunlight

A man is riding a slender camel, a woman
carrying a jar – two lives that give a human scale
to the empty landscape and open skies.
Their faces lack expression. Unspoken truths
and lies suggest a husband with his wife,
a king and his slave, strangers even.
The jar she offers him contains cold water
tasting of exhaustion or desire:
the words of greeting he will never speak
will never bring her peace.

The artist threads his needle, pulls tight,
bites off what isn't needed, spits
and then begins upon the same two lives again.
Beneath his fingers the wax-embroidered sun remains at noon;
the desert-sand raised up as darkness, catches fire.

Budapest: All Wars Are Civil Wars

The unfamiliar names of things soon blur
when I'm alone. I'm standing on a balcony;
nearby a church bell sounds the hour's surrender.
It's evening. History clings to every moment here:
bullets, hand-grenades and mortar-shells
have gouged their foreign script into the walls.

The Earth is tilting further from the sun
till east and west are forced into the one same
shadow. Night divides into a map of years
whose territories are now the street below
reaching to the far side of the world:
I stretch my hand into the dark to greet
whoever's there.

All things stand everywhere complete:
the church bell's silence marks a pause
between the past and future;
I touch the earth and feel its weight.

An Incident in Paris

Opposite, a light was burning;
in the flat nextdoor a clock chimed.
Every sense and nerve was lacerated.

A room in Paris: a dressing-table, a carpet
and matching curtains, make-up, clothes, a bed,
the girl I'd met earlier that evening.

Afterwards I glance across the street.
The light has been switched off, the clock has stopped
striking: I am healing too quickly.

The Lake at Preda

The stream had ended in a glacier-green transparency of cloud, blue sky and mountain-shadow. We sat down,

shared our wedding-breakfast listening to the water's rush become accumulated stillness.

*

When we return next month the stream will have been silenced into ice, and the lake hardened.

The scene of our true wedding will become a sounding-board set between high mountains:
safe enough to stand on, jump on, dance on.

When we return – what winter-music we will make!

Barcelona: August Tenth

Sunlight cuts into the terrace where I'm sitting.

I speak your name aloud, expecting – what?
You are not here, nor ever coming here.

Love alters nothing but ourselves.

I want to raise my hand in farewell, nothing more.
Surely I do not have to move the sun
to mark a new beginning?

What I Remember Most

Your heart was the given heart.

Mine had long ago been hammered into place.

We listened, pretending the beats were counting out *one life, one life, one life...*

*

10am, and we were still awake.
Morning couldn't reach us. Our love-heat,
no more than mist upon the windows now, had stopped the sun
from entering your room.

*

Since you've asked I'll tell you what I remember most:

We're dressed. We're standing close together. It's time I left.
I feel the usual awkwardness, and wish
we'd kissed goodbye already and I'd gone –
for that is how our past anticipates, is lived out
and a life is done.
Just then you give the steamed-up glass a wipe
to clear it. This could be my chance:

A show of wounded feelings, shocked
politeness. Anger. I'll tell you that our night
is not to be so easily erased.
Not for me at least.
The perfect exit line, then off.
I'm ready to deliver when you catch my eye –
you're smiling.

*

A moment's misunderstanding, you might say —
but it had lasted all my life.

You have to place your hand upon my shoulder.
You have to turn me round to make me look again.
How long does it take until I understand
and feel my heart breaking
at last?

For that's what I remember most: your given heart,
and mine released to see the busy street outside,
to see the city where we will live.

Advertisement for a Scottish Servant

Would you like a very Scottish servant all your own
who'll do for, spiritually speaking, you alone?
A lad o' pairts: a prophet, historian and more,
a therapist/composer who understands the score?
Guaranteed – your past and future contrapuntally combined
into a pre-determined present so defined
you'll never need to think or feel again!

Your gardener for life, his motto: prune first then restrain
the slightest sign of growth. He'll cut you down to size
(for your own good) then train your roots to do
their darkest: dig deep, grasp, immobilise;
if needs be, split your soul in two.
He'll anticipate your every beck and call –
he *kent your faither*, after all!

As a Scottish-school economist he takes great pains
where pain was never due. No credit-giving Keynes,
he soon has Adam Smith's close-fistedness outclassed
insisting every childhood trauma last
your lifetime. All you'll need to know is what he'll tell you,
even when you're sleeping he'll compel you
treat his dreams as if they were your own.

Say 'Yes' – he's yours! Your very own: flesh, blood and bone
passed on as Scottish fathers pass him on
to Scottish sons (with references supplied
unto the seventh generation). A tendency to patricide
but nothing serious – just words – so never heed him.
This very Scottish servant –
who needs him?

One Life

1

Once when I was young I reached into the fire
from longing to possess the colours there.

2

I am the fire I'm reaching into now.
I grasp at flames and burn:
I am the colours that one by one return.

Today

Today I'm practising piano, a Chopin waltz.
A neighbour's dog starts barking so
I hammer even harder, *con fuoco*,
on the keys. Lunchtime drunks join in;
an out-of-tempo siren passes clawing
at each phrase. Meanwhile, two floors below,
ghetto-blasters measure out the bass.
Today the dead are thrust into their rightful place.

A Final Word on the Dream-house

Here is the house I lived in once: another man's house
another man's dream.

These are the rooms that obeyed him. The corridor's length
is witness to the tone he spoke in;
the banister-rail is edged with sunlight – his knuckles
clenching to hold the dream-house together.

Only those we've forgiven can die –
let this be a final word on the dream-house.

The Shadow-sailor

1

He's quite at sea (*that*, at least, is true).
By day he plays the captain and the crew
with rank and medals tattooed on –
gentle pinpricks cutting to the bone.
By night the empty crow's nest sways
between the cold moon and himself, and weighs
out stillness for the darkened scene below
letting the slightest measure only, flow
into his sea-crazed mind.

A tightened grip upon the helm and steering blind
he navigates by will-power, shapes
the changing waves according to a map
long out of date and precious. Ink-blots, tears and scrawls
mean 'Danger – hidden reef', 'cross-currents', 'rip-tide',
'wreckage'. Sea-wraiths advise him. Ghost-ships glide
through his, each unsounded passage falls
shadowless across his decks and hull.
He shuts his eyes to ward off the invisible.

2

He's more than halfway round his lifetime's only world:
to north and south the cries of drowning men
have turned to ice;
to east and west the ocean and the sun
dissolve into each other.

It's time to voyage further: to see what lies
beyond this shadow-sea, these shadow-skies.

It's time to take into himself the heavens'
own creation and destruction:

to make, of stars and minerals,
the darkness his imagination spills
unearthly light upon.

The Landscape We Live In

There is no bridge, there is no river –

The path no longer reaches to the hill –

The silver birch becomes a clutch of splintered branches –

Above us, a bird has paused with its wings outstretched.
How long before the sun itself ceases to move
unless we force it?

Lifeline

A certain woman takes my hand in hers to trace,
as best she can, the lines (some broken, some
complete) upon my skin. Signs, she tells me,
of the man I have become.

For the first time in my life I flinch in pain –
this open wound slashed long ago
across my palm.

A Ballad: In My House

Here in my house as I come and go
I meet echoes and shadows of no one I know.
We say echo-words, we play shadow-games:
no one hears them or sees them but I know their names.

I know where they live when they are alone
in the echo-and-shadow house all of their own.
They tell me their secrets and I tell them mine
but we tell on one else (not a word, not a sign) –

for these echoes break silence without making a sound,
and these shadows write darkness invisibly down.

Edinburgh: A Place of My Own

If I had sat outside the Caledonian Hotel
this afternoon, cross-legged on the pavement,
with the restaurant wall behind me –

If I had placed a plastic cup in front of me
and a blanket round
my shoulders –

If the hours had been the east wind cutting
the length of Lothian Road, while
the cold hardened into me –

If the day could not have been different, or the date
or the clouds or the sleet
or the rain –

If I'd stopped looking round me at faces,
at people; if I'd stopped staring down
at my uncovered hands –

If I had been sitting up straight
when they asked me to move –

If I'd still been sitting up straight when they touched
my shoulders to wake me –

*

A woman. A plastic cup. A blanket.
The pavement.
The wall.

They told her she had to move on.
She said nothing.
They asked her her name.
She said nothing.

*

If a sheet had been used to cover my face –
If the post-code for where I'd been begging
were tagged to my foot –

That post-code would have to stand for my name
when, at last, I'd be given a place of my own.

Prayer

When I reach the centre of the earth
let there be someone with me.
All things must bear the world's weight
but not alone.

So, when I return at last to this same hour
and this same place,
let there be someone raising
even the emptiness in his hands towards me.

Day and Night

By day my heart's a language I cannot speak.
My house is exile. Here is my empty hand;
here is when I next draw breath.

By night we find stars set in our hair,
in our eyes, in our skin –
and cannot stop the darkness rushing in.

The Present King of France

Even in her absence I am held here
by my fascination for the play. The scenery
and seasons are each a metaphor
for what's unspoken in the script,
what's happening off-stage.

During the interval a gin and tonic
will refresh me. During my performance
I will drink for real. In the next scene
I become the present King of France,
and she the Queen.

Until then I have nothing to say,
and no *business* here. Books
are on the shelves; art on the wall.
Too many plants. Sunlight
invades a corner of the room.

I've sat here for the last hour staring
at the plants, the sunlight
and the art. I've followed her
across the city; watched her
hail a taxi, paused

with her in front of window-displays
checking her appearance.
Her green velvet skirt brings out a colour
in her eyes I have not seen
for a long, long time.

Note: The phrase 'the present king of France' comes from Bertrand Russell's essay *On Denoting* which discusses the idea that words might have a meaning to someone and yet have no answering reference in the real world. Like in the case of one-sided love, for example.

When I read time passes slowly.
I become tired. When I drink
time does not pass at all –
I no longer need books, or drink
or anything...

*

What will the present King of France need –
to rule others? To order 'Kneel',
'Arise', and watch some courtier
(or queen) go down upon
one knee then up, seems even duller

than watching my glass empty and fill.
A thousand courtiers would be
more amusing – being a thousand times more
absurd. A thousand glasses?
Who's counting? The Queen

already plays her part with skill
if not with understanding – I must
play mine. 'To every action
there is an equal and opposite
reaction' – that's the law.

Should I invite Newton to Versailles?
An indifferent conversationalist,
I'm told. Should I command an afternoon
passed beside the lake? Once out of this house
might I find myself closer

to what Newton and the Queen cannot
explain away...?

*

For her an afternoon's enjoyment means
deceit. At lunch she kissed me.
I kissed her in return –
the deceiver is so easily
deceived.

She wore the bracelets I had given her –
hammered silver, six of them.
At lunch I counted seven. I recognised
the different sound they made.
I counted them. I can count.

*

The next scene is about to start.
I must prepare. The present King of France
need hardly beg an audience;
it is he who will give audience
to her. To her deceits.

When I say I love her I will look
into her eyes and hope:
that she will not stumble over her reply
or keep the house embarrassed
with a silence.

        For nothing
can erase the slightest hesitation
that one day
answers the words:
'I love you.'

A prop misplaced from another scene (that bracelet
of hammered silver, for example) undermines
the whole performance. It should be
palmed from sight, or brought
into the action.

The less experienced actor struggles on, pretending
nothing's changed, persisting
in lines already made ridiculous.
The greater actor raises himself
above deception.

I love her, and know that love is not
enough. From now on,
our play concerns a king's love
for his queen: the everyday
as metaphor for something greater

and more vulnerable...

*

When the interval is over these shadows
will become the shadows cast
along the palace colonnade;

the taste of gin become the tone
her voice takes for her entrance.
She leans upon my arm:

'Be served only by those you know
to be corrupt.' How well she understands
her power, and mine.

When the sun goes down upon the lake
we will speak of other matters,
but too briefly...

Three Biographies

This morning. The weather. The bus. What is outside
is out of focus: the Clarke Road shops are blown across
the glass as rain; streetlights smear.

A man's hand touches the side of his face
every few seconds. Next to him
a girl, whose fair hair's much too short
to be comfortably looked at, chews
and stares. Next again, is me.

Three biographies all up to date:
we turn the page, read on (our dreams alone
our own responsibility).

The traffic stops. It's dark enough to see my likeness
looking in: mid-forties grey to silver-
grey. He's caught my eye.

He'd like to smile, and does;
he'd like to reach his hand towards mine,
make contact. Be *sure*.

*

There are spirits trapped outside us,
we keep them at arm's length or
beyond. Their image caught on glass:
a spell conjuring who we are
as if from nothing; and our lives,
the small enchantment that remains.

What we know is what we fear we have to lose.

No mark upon the man's skin,
no sign of pain...
The girl's nailed-in hair,
her hands' stillness, her perfume...

What we fear is what we know will break the spell.

The bus jerks forwards: Clarke Road,
the rain, the filthy window.

Our histories continue out of sight.

Letting the Demons Speak
(for Roger, and Anja)

1 *The Carry-out Calendar*

The usual picture: two Chinese men, a tea-house,
path, a mountain with its cloud (top right) as if
to post the early evening far into the future.

No background, but then there never is.
The unpainted parts between the tea-house
and the mountain, the mountain

and the cloud, remind us (once
we've phoned our order in, of course,
and have to wait

and wait) of how the infinite surrounds
man's every moment, or the eternal
something...

Anja-Time, that metaphysics of pure greed complemented
by complete forgiveness, repeats one life
over between sleeps.

Two bottles and sufficient cognac will remove the background
to *our* evening also: every top-up helps us
paint out a little more.

That's where the demons are: hiding just beyond the first,
the second and every glass, and coming nearer;
reshaping Time into a series of concentric moments set
to trap us at the centre.

Elsewhere, the Scottish Tao: say nothing
until you're sure it is too late;
do nothing until you're sure there's nothing
can be done. The Scottish Way is – no way.

And so, two Scottish men, two Chinese men
twelve hundred years apart, sit down together
to let the demons speak.

2 *Anja*

Thursday evening. 6pm. Anja barks the flat into an urgency:

The streetdoor's banging shut is followed once,

                twice,

thrice,

    by the faintest...
                then less faint...
                            step
                                  by
                                      step
                              as every step
                      proves...
              not...
        to be...
    the last:

Three floors down the messenger's begun his 47-stair ascent –
and Anja *knows*.

                *

(Once upon a time she visited the Eastern Pearl:
Its door pushed open, she entered no longer walking
upon the surface of the earth...

... As we left she barked to the effect that our departure was,
essentially, a banishment, a return to Plato's cave.
The shadow-crackers cooling in the plastic bag would taste,

she added, of exile and greater longing.)

                *

She cannot wait for lesser beings' single speed to catch her up:

She herds the slowest seconds into a flock
She barks them
                     She whines them
                                      She harries them around
the table legs and chairs
                            She chases them into the hall
                                              Clockwise
                       round the brolly stand and back
        until they're penned in
    and done with
instantly.

She's at the door now, glaring across the gap between us
and the future she's already reached (*there*,
the bell's been rung, the meal delivered).

3 *My friend and I*

The two of us meanwhile (too-human, therefore trapped
in a continuum of four dimensions seen
as three)
must plod our one way at our one speed
towards the dresser and the draining-board (landmarks
on our journey through time)
collecting souvenirs, arranging them
(these articles of our remaining faith in any remaining future)
upon the kitchen table: the plates, bowls, chopsticks,
wine, the Chinese teapot, napkins, place-mats,
glasses, cups.

The corkscrew.

*

The doorbell rings. The Eastern Pearl delivery resolves
both dog-barked time, and our conventional delay.
We pay. Unwrap.
Sit down.

The demons would prefer we gossiped, talked politics
or art (three very demon-topics
certainly discussed in ancient China).

Gossip: Speaking of someone else's pain to ease our own.

Politics: Our deepest fears recycled as conviction.

Art: Renouncing our demons and ourselves,
briefly.

Instead: Some Opus 20 Haydn, spring rolls and the first Rioja.

4 *The Meal Begins*

There are no demons in the tea-house, at least
none visible. The bamboo door's slid open: one man's leaning

forward as if to stress a point he's made, or hear
exactly what's been said. The other's attitude remains

unclear: he's been badly printed, no more
than a smudge across the table.

*

(Anja's no dog-noun anymore. A mouth, a highly active verb beneath
the table: *Waiting*.

An alertness of fur and ear and eye: *Stretching*

towards a truth so far beyond us
as to taste of blasphemy...

For her, the here and now's restored as one,

       two,

three gobbled-down crackers)

*

My friend sits opposite; nearby a second bottle breathes
on our behalf. The pause between two Haydn movements sets
a frame of sudden silence round us:

Brushstrokes never made upon the invisibility of silk
show us all that is not here and all
that is – within the clenching of our hearts.
Elsewhere, metaphor and imitation: nothing
in our lives accepted merely for what it is,
ourselves included.
Elsewhere, the telephone rings, a letter arrives –
we grow older and more afraid.

So, more wine, another aluminium trough of lemon chicken!
Here come the demons.
Welcome.

Ryecroft
(in memory of my mother who died 4th November 1991)

1 *Departures*

My mother died much slower than expected:
I saw her, talked, held her hands, sat,
held her hands, kissed goodbye
and left the nursing home. That visit lasted seven months.

Soon it will be March. We have returned to work on Ryecroft:
a front door of hardwood panels crumbling
to yellow dampness;
a backdoor of corrugated metal hammered
onto rotten planks.
The window frames and ceilings are secured by clouded stillness
gathered into filth around the bundled-up dead.
Uncurtained daylight chills me.

There has been no winter until now:
a bedroom already hardened into ice around
a hairbrush, comb, kleenex, photographs and her
stiffening face upon the pillow.

2 *Beginnings*

Destruction must come first, and second and third:
a chisel and steel toe-caps to the sagging floors and skirting;
a sledgehammer to the fireplace whose brickwork flinches
when it's touched;
bare hands to the ribcage laths and plaster.
Everything shovelled up and wheelbarrowed outside.

2174 slates are stripped off: a century's darkness lifts
for an afternoon. There's the slightest catch of breath
as every one of 2174 nails is drawn out.
The skylight, a bloodshot and corroded eye rusted half open,
is plucked out with a crowbar.

The garden (on neighbourly advice) will be poisoned
into submission.

3 *Walking Together*

Before my mother starts her journey home
she has to rest a moment:
last week we reached the fence beside the railway line,
today we've come no further than the yellow bush.

When I feel her touch upon my arm I know
she's ready to turn back. She doesn't smile:
grasping her stick as tightly as she can she moves
forwards, testing the ground at every step.

4 *The Rats*

Their sky was laid out in planks with hardly a Rizla-paper's gap
between each tongue and groove. Underneath,
a black sea without tide, night without day;
where the floor was badly wormholed stars began. Is this
the rats' astronomy? Does the rate of wood decay
when set against the lifespan of a rat allow
a glimpse of the eternal?

Those who've read their futures in the wormwood
have hurriedly moved on; the rest will see the light too late.
A firm tug. The lino lifts. New heavens blaze
above them...

...Afterwards I hammer-claw the lengths of sky for burning:
the rustiest nails snap cleanly;
the best – Excaliburs eased out in one.

5 *This year*

As the days grew shorter we'd sing our way home through darkness –
her voice in front, mine half a step behind.
Trees clawed at us and the wind hissed –
I held her coat tight.

This year we keep to the concrete path around the building.
Tea and biscuits in her room. A bed, a chair, radio,
some photographs; she says she's everything she needs.

Another day has passed, another evening. I'll leave soon.
I have to. When the trees press too close our hands touch:

There is no singing, no road home.

6 The Bath

Standing in the middle of a field: claw-footed,
white-lipped, porcelain-plungered, fully stretched
for the reading of detective novels in;
ocean-going, and of Jurassic proportions
all but extinct in this designer-world.

Less than two miles from the river Annan. There was mud
to walk through, thistles, nettles and cows to avoid;
barbed wire to climb over. A cloudless sky:
the sun had a perfect view of me the day
I first climbed in, trying it for size.

7 *The Curtains Were Closed*

The curtains were closed when I entered her room:
the day was shut out, the night was shut out
and she wasn't there.

I looked down at her face, her mouth and her eyes:
I tried to remember her mouth and her eyes.

The walls were as mist when mist disappears,
the door falling rain that no longer falls;

the corridor ran the length of the world
and she wasn't there.

8 Clambering Up

These rafters, dirt and cobwebs will be turned
to sunlight on varnished wood.
No staircase yet. I'll help you clamber up.
I'll fight off spiders.

The trapdoor hinge sticks. Wrenching the metal back
I touch the coldness of my mother's hand.
I feel her fingers claw the air in front of her.
I kneel beside her bed until her weightlessness becomes

your smile, your red hair drawn up into my arms a moment past.
This is the beginning of winter and of spring.
We pause for breath. In dreams alone there is finality:

I hold you both as tightly as I can.

Ron Butlin was born in 1949 in Edinburgh, grew up in Dumfriesshire, and studied at Edinburgh University (where he took an MA and postgraduate diploma in Adult Education).

Since 1979 he has been a full-time writer, with seven books published. His poetry and fiction have won three Scottish Arts Council Book Awards and a Poetry Book Society Recommendation.

He has edited numerous anthologies of adults' and children's work, and judged several writing competitions. He is an occasional reviewer for *The Scotsman*, television and radio.

Besides his radio plays much of his work has been broadcast in Britain and abroad. His poetry and fiction have been translated into over ten languages. He has participated in major literary festivals in Edinburgh, London, Toronto and Paris, and has given readings in Russia, Eastern Europe, North America, Nigeria, Mauritius and Australia.

As well as gaining several SAC Writers' Bursaries, he has been Writer in Residence at Edinburgh University, University of New Brunswick (Canada), University of Stirling, for Midlothian Libraries and Lothian Region Education Department. He has over fifteen years' experience in running writing groups at all levels for local authorities, WEA, Arvon and university extra-mural departments.

At present he is completing his third novel. He lives in Edinburgh with his wife and their dog.